Vegan Smoothies to Go: Quick and Easy Vegan Recipes That Are Ready When You Are

All rights Reserved. No part of this publication or the information in it may be quoted from or reproduced in any form by means such as printing, scanning, photocopying or otherwise without prior written permission of the copyright holder.

Disclaimer and Terms of Use: Effort has been made to ensure that the information in this book is accurate and complete, however, the author and the publisher do not warrant the accuracy of the information, text and graphics contained within the book due to the rapidly changing nature of science, research, known and unknown facts and Internet. The Author and the publisher do not hold any responsibility for errors, omissions or contrary interpretation of the subject matter herein. This book is presented solely for motivational and informational purposes only.

Table of Contents

Coconut Cream 5

Watermelon Dandelion 6

Acai Smoothie 7

Mango Smoothie 8

Blue Beets 9

Green Apple Smoothie 10

Apple Flaxseed Smoothie 11

Sour Lemonade 12

Arugula Smoothie 13

Fig Smoothie 14

Pina Colada Smoothie 15

Soy Smoothie 16

Chia Smoothie 17

Revitalizer Smoothie 18

Creamy Pomegranate Smoothie 19

Chocolate Almond Smoothie 20

Plum Smoothie 21

Blueberry Nuts Smoothie 22

Key Lime Smoothie 23

Honeydew Smoothie 24

Pumpkin Chia Smoothie 25

Kiwi Smoothie 26

Tropical Vegan Smoothie 27

All Green 28

Blue Sky Smoothie 29

Coconut Cream

Ingredients:
- 1 C Thai coconut water
- Coconut shreds (from small coconut)
- 1 tsp. coconut oil
- ½ C mango chunks
- ½ tsp vanilla powder
- Ice
- ½ C blueberries

Directions:

I. Start by adding everything into your blender or food processor
II. Blend everything on medium to high, until well blended
III. Serve

Watermelon Dandelion

Ingredients:
- ½ C water
- 1 C watermelon
- ½ tsp turmeric
- ½ T grated ginger
- ½ T lemon juice
- 1 banana
- Honey

Directions:

I. Start by adding everything into your blender or food processor
II. Blend everything on medium to high, until well blended
III. Serve

Acai Smoothie

Ingredients:
- 1 C coconut water
- 1 T acai powder
- 1/2 c blueberries
- Ice
- 1 C kale
- 1/3 C goji berries
- 1 T cacao
- 1 T honey

Directions:

I. Start by adding everything into your blender or food processor
II. Blend everything on medium to high, until well blended
III. Serve

Mango Smoothie

Ingredients:
- 1 C coconut water
- 1 T acai powder
- 1 C mango chunks
- 1 banana
- Honey
- ½ C pineapple, chunks
- 1 T chia seeds

Directions:

I. Start by adding everything into your blender or food processor
II. Blend everything on medium to high, until well blended
III. Serve

Blue Beets

Ingredients:
- 1 C almond water
- 1 apple, cored
- ½ C blueberries
- 2 T ground flaxseed

Directions:

I. Start by adding everything into your blender or food processor
II. Blend everything on medium to high, until well blended
III. Serve

Green Apple Smoothie

Ingredients:
- 1 C apple juice
- 1 cored apple
- ½ C strawberries
- 1 C baby spinach
- 1 tsp coconut oil
- ½ C blueberries
- ½ T maca

Directions:

I. Start by adding everything into your blender or food processor
II. Blend everything on medium to high, until well blended
III. Serve

Apple Flaxseed Smoothie

Ingredients:
- 1 C apple
- 1 apple, cored
- ½ C blueberries
- 2 T flaxseed
- ¼ C yogurt

Directions:

I. Start by adding everything into your blender or food processor
II. Blend everything on medium to high, until well blended
III. Serve

Sour Lemonade

Ingredients:
- 1 C water
- 1 seeded apple
- 1 lemon
- 1 tsp coconut oil
- 1 tsp honey

Directions:

I. Start by adding everything into your blender or food processor
II. Blend everything on medium to high, until well blended
III. Serve

Arugula Smoothie

Ingredients:
- 1 C coconut water
- ½ C arugula
- ½ C spinach
- 1 banana
- 1 tsp coconut oil
- ½ C strawberries
- ½ C blueberries

Directions:

I. Start by adding everything into your blender or food processor
II. Blend everything on medium to high, until well blended
III. Serve

Fig Smoothie

Ingredients:
- 1 mango, chopped
- 1 banana chopped
- 1 T oats
- ½ T macadamia nuts
- 1 soy milk
- ½ tsp yogurt
- 1 tsp chia seeds

Directions:

I. Start by adding everything into your blender or food processor
II. Blend everything on medium to high, until well blended
III. Serve

Pina Colada Smoothie

Ingredients:
- 1 can crushed pineapple
- 1 C coconut milk
- 3 bananas
- Shredded coconut

Directions:

I. Start by adding everything into your blender or food processor
II. Blend everything on medium to high, until well blended
III. Serve

Soy Smoothie

Ingredients:
- 1 ½ C Almond milk
- 1 banana
- ½ tsp green tea
- 1 T chia seeds
- 1 S Stevia extract

Directions:

I. Start by adding everything into your blender or food processor
II. Blend everything on medium to high, until well blended
III. Serve

Chia Smoothie

Ingredients:
- 1 ½ C almond milk
- 1 banana
- ½ tsp matcha

Directions:

I. Start by adding everything into your blender or food processor
II. Blend everything on medium to high, until well blended
III. Serve

Revitalizer Smoothie

Ingredients:
- 1 ½ C almond milk
- 1 C strawberries
- 1 S protein powder
- ¼ C almonds
- 1 coconut oil
- 1 T maca powder
- 1 T hemp seeds

Directions:

I. Start by adding everything into your blender or food processor
II. Blend everything on medium to high, until well blended
III. Serve

Creamy Pomegranate Smoothie

Ingredients:
- 1 C pomegranate seeds
- ½ C coconut milk
- 1 T chia seeds
- 1 C chopped greens
- Ice

Directions:

I. Start by adding everything into your blender or food processor
II. Blend everything on medium to high, until well blended
III. Serve

Chocolate Almond Smoothie

Ingredients:
- 1 ½ C almond milk
- 1 C blueberries
- 1 C chocolate whey powder
- 1 C almonds softened
- 1 coconut oil
- 1 T hemp seeds

Directions:

I. Start by adding everything into your blender or food processor
II. Blend everything on medium to high, until well blended
III. Serve

Plum Smoothie

Ingredients:
- ½ C almond milk
- 1 C water
- 2 T chia seeds
- 1 T coconut oil
- ¼ tsp pumpkin pie
- ¼ tsp ginger
- 1 ½ plum bites
- ½ C chopped raw
- ½ C ice

Directions:

I. Start by adding everything into your blender or food processor
II. Blend everything on medium to high, until well blended
III. Serve

Blueberry Nuts Smoothie

Ingredients:
- Cashews
- Water
- 1 mango, chopped
- 1 C blueberries
- ¼ C ice
- 1 T chia seeds
- 1 T oats
- 1 T honey

Directions:

I. Start by adding everything into your blender or food processor
II. Blend everything on medium to high, until well blended
III. Serve

Key Lime Smoothie

Ingredients:
- 2 C coconut water
- ¼ C lime juice
- 1 avocado
- ¼ C shredded coconut shreds
- ¼ C spinach leaves
- Ice

Directions:

I. Start by adding everything into your blender or food processor
II. Blend everything on medium to high, until well blended
III. Serve

Honeydew Smoothie

Ingredients:
- 2 C honeydew
- 2 C almond milk
- Ice

Directions:

I. Start by adding everything into your blender or food processor
II. Blend everything on medium to high, until well blended
III. Serve

Pumpkin Chia Smoothie

Ingredients:
- 3/4 C almond milk
- 1/2 C black tea
- 1/2 C pumpkin puree
- 1/2 C silken tofu
- 1/2 T maple syrup
- 1/2 tsp vanilla
- 1/2 tsp cinnamon
- 1/4 tsp ground ginger
- 1/8 tsp cardamom

Directions:

I. Start by adding everything into your blender or food processor
II. Blend everything on medium to high, until well blended
III. Serve

Kiwi Smoothie

Ingredients:
- 1/2 avocado
- 2 kiwis
- 1/8 C lime juice
- 1/4 C almond milk
- Honey
- Ice

Directions:

I. Start by adding everything into your blender or food processor
II. Blend everything on medium to high, until well blended
III. Serve

Tropical Vegan Smoothie

Ingredients:
- 1 kiwi
- ½ C pineapple
- 1 C coconut milk
- 1 T chopped nuts
- ½ C chopped mango
- Ice

Directions:

I. Start by adding everything into your blender or food processor
II. Blend everything on medium to high, until well blended
III. Serve

All Green

Ingredients:
- 1 Green apple, cored
- 1 C Kale
- 1 C baby spinach
- ¼ tsp coconut flakes
- 1 C almond milk
- 1 T Whey powder
- Ice

Directions:

I. Start by adding everything into your blender or food processor
II. Blend everything on medium to high, until well blended
III. Serve

Blue Sky Smoothie

Ingredients:
- 1 C blueberries
- 1 C almond milk
- ¼ C shredded coconut flakes
- Ice

Directions:

I. Start by adding everything into your blender or food processor
II. Blend everything on medium to high, until well blended
III. Serve

Printed in Great Britain
by Amazon